To:

From: Karen

Friends Make the Best Presents

Written and compiled by
Holly Stevens

Illustrated by Sandy Haight

PETER PAUPER PRESS, INC.
White Plains, New York

Illustrations copyright
© 2005 Sandy Haight

Designed by Taryn R. Sefecka

Copyright © 2005
Peter Pauper Press, Inc.
202 Mamaroneck Avenue
White Plains, NY 10601

ISBN 978-1-59359-902-7
Printed in China
14 13 12 11 10 9 8

Visit us at www.peterpauper.com

INTRODUCTION

I t's been said that the greatest gifts come in small packages, but in fact, the very best gifts don't come in packages at all!

You needn't live as long as Santa Claus to know that Friends make the best presents. After all, 'tis the season to be jolly, and who better to be jolly with than your good friends?

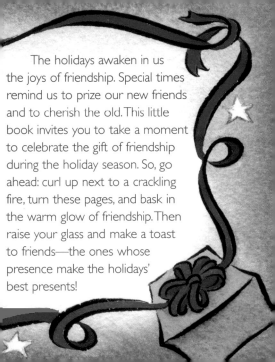

The holidays awaken in us the joys of friendship. Special times remind us to prize our new friends and to cherish the old. This little book invites you to take a moment to celebrate the gift of friendship during the holiday season. So, go ahead: curl up next to a crackling fire, turn these pages, and bask in the warm glow of friendship. Then raise your glass and make a toast to friends—the ones whose presence make the holidays' best presents!

Remember, the greatest gift is not found in a store nor under a tree, but in the hearts of true friends.

CINDY LEW

In a friend
you find
a second self.

ISABELLE NORTON

You'll have the
whole world in
your hands if you
can count a friend
on each finger.

The only gift is a portion of thyself.

RALPH WALDO EMERSON

Friends can laugh at each other—and at themselves!

Walking with a friend in the dark is better than walking alone in the light.

HELEN KELLER

Friends . . . cherish one another's hopes. They are kind to one another's dreams.

HENRY DAVID THOREAU

Lots of people want
to ride with you in the limo,
but what you want is
someone who will take the
bus with you when the
limo breaks down.

OPRAH WINFREY

We may live on
separate shores,
but in the end,
we're all in
the same boat.

Like a good book,
a lasting friendship
has many chapters.

A comfortable
silence shared by
friends speaks
volumes.

To your enemy, forgiveness.
To an opponent, tolerance.
To a friend, your heart.
To a customer, service.
To all, charity. To every
child, a good example.
To yourself, respect.

OREN ARNOLD

Familiarity
breeds content.

ANNA QUINDLEN

True friends delight in each other's successes.

My friends and the people around me have never changed and I am immensely grateful for that.

KATE WINSLET

If you wish
to have a friend,
be a friend.

The roaring brook, the whispering pine, the cooing birds, a friend by your side.

A true friend
is there for the
ups as well as
the downs.

Hug a friend and
embrace one of life's
simplest pleasures.

Friendship is
knowing the right
thing to say, and
knowing when
it's right to say
nothing at all.

To share your thoughts with a trusted friend is to double your happiness and halve your troubles.

A friend is
a gift you
give yourself.

ROBERT LOUIS STEVENSON

A friend is there for your "aha!" moments and all the moments in between.

One is taught by experience
to put a premium on those
few people who can appreciate
you for what you are.

GAIL GODWIN

Raise your glass and make a toast to friends—the ones whose presence make the holidays' best presents.

Friends
outlast
trends.

Loyalty is the cement that seals the bonds of friendship.

To dwell on a
friend's mistake
is to make a
second mistake.

Friends are
gold threads
in the fabric
of life.

If all the world's a stage, cast your friends in leading roles.

With a good friend, you don't have to be "on" when you're feeling "off."

A true friend is the best possession.

BEN FRANKLIN

You see only your
most beautiful
self reflected
in the eyes of
a true friend.

Friendship is always a sweet responsibility, never an opportunity.

KAHLIL GIBRAN

One loyal friend is worth ten thousand relatives.

EURIPIDES

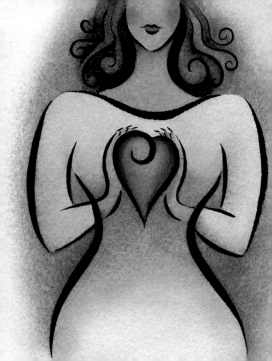

Accept affection
with open arms,
and give it with
an open heart.

Friendship . . . is not something you learn in school. But if you haven't learned the meaning of friendship, you really haven't learned anything.

MUHAMMAD ALI

An achievement is
so much sweeter when
you celebrate it with
a good friend.

A friend listens to
what you say. A good
friend listens to what
you don't say.

Sometimes the
most valuable
thing a friend
can lend is
a ready ear.

Those who bring
sunshine to the lives
of others cannot keep
it from themselves.

JAMES M. BARRIE

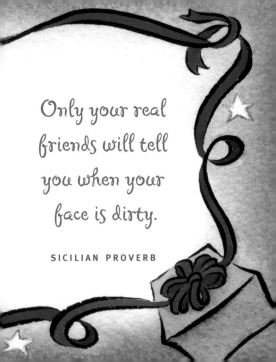

Only your real friends will tell you when your face is dirty.

SICILIAN PROVERB

Only a life lived for others is a life worthwhile.

ALBERT EINSTEIN

In friendship,
the more you
give, the richer
you grow.

A true friend is
someone who thinks
that you are a good egg
even though he
knows that you are
slightly cracked.

BERNARD MELTZER

Friendship endures over time even when the content of that friendship changes.

Love is the only force
capable of transforming
an enemy into friend.

MARTIN LUTHER KING, JR.

Prize your
new friends,
and cherish
the old.

Be a friend
and you'll
have a friend.

You are twice blessed if you can travel the journey of life with a true friend.

A lasting friendship is marked less by a sprinkling of grand gestures and more by a long stream of small kindnesses.

The best friends are
like diamonds;
treasure them and
they will sparkle.

Friendships, like good wine, need time to age before one can savor and enjoy their flavor.

A good friend
is someone who
lends a helping
hand in times
of need.

Friends are the family we choose.

JENNIFER ANISTON

True friendship
ought never
to conceal what
it thinks.

ST. JEROME

Plant a seed of
friendship;
reap a bouquet
of happiness.

LOIS L. KAUFMAN

What I cannot love, I overlook. Is that real friendship?

ANAÏS NIN

One true
friend is worth a
hundred casual
acquaintances.

A hug is a great gift—
one size fits all, and
it's easy to exchange.

AUTHOR UNKNOWN

Too often we underestimate
the power of a touch, a smile,
a kind word, a listening ear,
an honest compliment, or
the smallest act of caring,
all of which have the potential
to turn a life around.

LEO BUSCAGLIA

Good
friends are
forever.

The gift of
friendship is
the gift of
a lifetime.

The road of life
is a lot less bumpy
with good friends
along for the ride.

Do not save your loving speeches for your friends till they are dead. Do not write them on their tombstones; speak them rather now instead.

ANNA CUMMINS